Creeds to Live By, Dreams to Follow

Creeds to Live By, Dreams to Follow

A collection of poems
Edited by Susan Polis Schutz

Blue Mountain Press ™

Boulder, Colorado

Library of Congress Catalog Card Number: 86-73018
ISBN: 0-88396-248-9

The following works have previously appeared in Blue Mountain Arts publications:

"If you know," by Susan Polis Schutz. Copyright © Continental Publications, 1978. "Many people," by Susan Polis Schutz. Copyright © Continental Publications, 1979. "Love Your Life," by Susan Polis Schutz. Copyright © Stephen Schutz and Susan Polis Schutz, 1982. "Believe in Yourself," by Sherrie Householder; "Love," by Barb Upham; and "If We Don't Take Chances, then We'll Never Find Rainbows," by Collin McCarty. Copyright © Blue Mountain Arts, Inc., 1986. "My Creed," by Laine Parsons; "You Can Soar Higher than You've Ever Dreamed," by Edmund O'Neill; "A Creed for Today and Every Day," by Anna Marie Edwards; "A Creed to Live By" and "There Is a Winner Inside Each of Us," by Nancye Sims; "Life's Most Important Treasures," by Maureen Doan; "May You Always Feel Loved," by Sandra Sturtz; and "Begin Again," "Hold on," "Don't put off living until tomorrow," "Each and every one of us," "Celebrate Life," and "If ever things begin to look a little cloudy . . . ," by Collin McCarty. Copyright © Blue Mountain Arts, Inc., 1987. All rights reserved.

Thanks to the Blue Mountain Arts creative staff.

ACKNOWLEDGMENTS appear on page 62.

Manufactured in the United States of America
First printing: February, 1987

Blue Mountain Press INC.

P.O. Box 4549, Boulder, Colorado 80306

CONTENTS

Believe in Yourself

*B*elieve that you have the destiny, the innate ability, to become all you expect of life. Experience all of life's peaks and plateaus. Find the meaning of life's struggles and accomplishments. There you will find the meaning to life and life's work.

Trust in your deeply hidden feelings, because they show the person that you are. Take hold of each opportunity, and make the most of it.

Know the person that you are, the needs that your life contains. Search deeply to capture the essence of life. Find your limitations and build upon them. Create within yourself a person who is strong and capable of withstanding pain.

Know that life will offer some disappointments, but remember, through those situations you become a stronger, more stable person. Don't overlook obstacles, but work through them. Remember that each road you choose will offer some difficulty. If life were meant to be easy, there would be no challenges and no rainbows.

— Sherrie Householder

A Creed to Live By

Don't undermine your worth
by comparing yourself with others.
It is because we are different
that each of us is special.
Don't set your goals by what
other people deem important.
Only you know what is best for you.
Don't take for granted the things
closest to your heart.
Cling to them as you would your life,
for without them life is meaningless.
Don't let your life slip through your fingers
by living in the past, or for the future.
By living your life one day at a time,
you live all the days of your life.
Don't give up when you still have
something to give.
Nothing is really over
until the moment you stop trying.
Don't be afraid to admit that
you are less than perfect.
It is this fragile thread
that binds us to each other.

Don't be afraid to encounter risks.
It is by taking chances that
we learn how to be brave.
Don't shut love out of your life
by saying it's impossible to find.
The quickest way to receive love
is to give love;
the fastest way to lose love
is to hold it too tightly;
and the best way to keep love
is to give it wings.
Don't dismiss your dreams.
To be without dreams is to be without hope;
to be without hope is to be without purpose.
Don't run through life so fast
that you forget not only where you've been
but also where you're going.
Life is not a race,
but a journey to be savored
each step of the way.

— Nancye Sims

Life's Most Important Treasures

Joy
in your heart,
your mind,
your soul.
Peace
with yourself
and with the universe.
Harmony.
Courage
to feel, to need,
to reach out.
Freedom
to let yourself
be bound by love.
Friendship.
Wisdom
to learn, to change,
to let go.
Acceptance
of the truth
and beauty within yourself.
Growth.
Pleasure
in all that you see,
and touch,
and do.
Happiness
with yourself
and with the world.
Love.

— Maureen Doan

Love

Love takes time. It needs a history of giving
and receiving, laughing and crying . . .
*Love never promises instant gratification, only
ultimate fulfillment.*
*Love means believing in someone, in
something. It supposes a willingness to
struggle, to work, to suffer, and to rejoice.*
*Satisfaction and ultimate fulfillment are
by-products of dedicated love. They belong only
to those who can reach beyond themselves; to
whom giving is more important than
receiving.*
*Love is doing everything you can to help others
build whatever dreams they have.*
*Love involves much careful and active listening.
It is doing whatever needs to be done, and
saving whatever will promote the other's
happiness, security, and well-being.
Sometimes, love hurts.*
*Love is on a constant journey to what others
need. It must be attentive, caring and open,
both to what others say and to what others
cannot say.*
*Love says no with empathy and great
compassion.*
Love is firm, but when needed it must be tender.

When others have tried and failed, love is the
   hand in yours in your moments of
   discouragement and disappointment.
Love is reliable.
Love is a choice and commitment to others' true
   and lasting happiness. It is dedicated to
   growth and fulfillment. Love is not selfish.
Love sometimes fails for lack of wisdom or
   abundance of weakness, but it forgives,
   knowing the intentions are good.
Love does not attach conditions . . . Genuine
   love is always a free gift.
Love realizes and accepts that there will be
   disagreements and disturbing emotions . . .
   There may be times when miles lay between,
   but love is a commitment. It believes, and
   endures all things.
Love encourages freedom of self. Love shares
   positive and negative reactions to warm and
   cold feelings.
Love, intimate love, will never reject others. It is
   the first to encourage and the last to condemn.
Love is a commitment to growth, happiness,
   and fulfillment of one another.

— Barb Upham

If We Don't Take Chances,
then We'll Never Find the Rainbows

If we don't ever take chances,
   we won't reach the rainbows.
If we don't ever search,
   we'll never be able to find.
If we don't attempt to get over
      our doubts and fears,
         we'll never discover how wonderful
            it is to live without them.
If we don't go beyond difficulty,
      we won't grow any stronger.
If we don't keep our dreams alive,
      we won't have our dreams any longer.

But . . .
if we can take a chance now and then,
seek and search, discover and dream,
grow and go through each day
with the knowledge that
we can only take as much as we can give,
and we can only get as much out of life
      as we allow ourselves to live . . .

Then . . .
we can be truly happy.
We can realize a dream or two along the way,
and we can make a habit of
      reaching out for rainbows
            and coloring our lives
                  with wonderful days.

— Collin McCarty

There Is a Winner Inside Each of Us

Winners take chances.
Like everyone else, they fear failing,
but they refuse to let fear control them.
Winners don't give up.
When life gets rough, they hang in
until the going gets better.
Winners are flexible.
They realize there is more than one way
and are willing to try others.
Winners know they are not perfect.
They respect their weaknesses
while making the most of their strengths.
Winners fall, but they don't stay down.
They stubbornly refuse to let a fall
keep them from climbing.
Winners don't blame fate for their failures
nor luck for their successes.
Winners accept responsibility for their lives.
Winners are positive thinkers
who see good in all things.
From the ordinary, they make the extraordinary.
Winners believe in the path they have chosen
even when it's hard,
even when others can't see where they are going.
Winners are patient.
They know a goal is only as worthy
as the effort that's required to achieve it.

— Nancye Sims

You Can Be Whatever You Want to Be

There is inside you
all of the potential to be whatever
  you want to be —
all of the energy to do whatever
  you want to do.
Imagine yourself as you would like to be,
  doing what you want to do,
and each day, take one step towards
  your dream.
And though at times it may seem too
  difficult to continue,
hold on to your dream.
One morning you will awake to find
that you are the person you dreamed of —
  doing what you wanted to do —
simply because you had the courage
to believe in your potential
and to hold on to your dream.

— *Donna Levine*

Love Your Life

We cannot
listen to what
others want us to do
We must listen
to ourselves
Society
family
friends
do not know what
we must do
Only we know
and only we
can do what is
right for us
So start right now
You will need to
work very hard

You will need to
overcome many obstacles
You will need to go
against the better
judgment of many people
and you will need to
bypass their prejudices
But you can have
whatever you want
if you try hard enough
So start right now and
you will live
a life designed
by you and for you
and you will
love your life

— Susan Polis Schutz

Begin Again

One of the best things we can do
in our lives is this: begin again.

Begin to see yourself as you were
   when you were the happiest
   and strongest you've ever been.

Begin to remember what worked for you
   (and what worked against you),
   and try to capture the magic again.

Begin to remember how natural it was
   when you were a child — to live
   a lifetime each day.

Begin to forget the baggage you have
   carried with you for years: the
   problems that don't matter anymore,
   the tears that cried themselves away,
   and the worries that are going to
   wash away on the shore of tomorrow's
   new beginning.

Tomorrow tells us it will be here
every new day of our lives; and
if we will be wise, we will turn
away from the problems of the past
and give the future
— and ourselves —
a chance to become the best of friends.

Sometimes all it takes
is a wish in the heart
to let yourself . . . begin again.

— Collin McCarty

*L*ife is our teacher,
teaching us with good experiences
and with painful ones.
The painful days are
difficult to understand,
but it is from these troubled times
that we learn how to be strong.
We learn to hold on and face
each day, even though we hurt
and feel frustrated.
We learn that the simplest pleasures
are often the most rewarding.
And we learn that losing is often
only another step towards winning.
And when life turns
its smiling side to us again,
as it always does,
we find ourselves stronger,
with a greater knowledge
of ourselves,
and able to feel the welcome comfort
of good times
more deeply than before.

— Donna Levine

May You Always Feel Loved

May you find serenity and tranquility in a world you may not always understand. May the pain you have known and the conflict you have experienced give you the strength to walk through life facing each new situation with courage and optimism. Always know that there are those whose love and understanding will always be there, even when you feel most alone. May you discover enough goodness in others to believe in a world of peace. May a kind word, a reassuring touch, and a warm smile be yours every day of your life, and may you give these gifts as well as receive them. Remember the sunshine when the storm seems unending. Teach love to those who know hate, and let that love embrace you as you go into the world. May the teachings of those you admire become part of you, so that you may call upon them. Remember, those whose lives you have touched and who have touched yours are always a part of you, even if the encounters were less than you would have wished. It is the content of the encounter that is more important than its form. May you not become too concerned with material matters, but instead place immeasurable value on the goodness in your heart. Find time in each day to see beauty and love in the world around you. Realize that each person has limitless abilities, but each of us is different in our own way. What you may feel you lack in one regard may be more than compensated for in another. What you feel you lack in the present may become one of your strengths in the future. May you see your future as one filled with promise and possibility. Learn to view everything as a worthwhile experience. May you find enough inner strength to determine your own worth by yourself, and not be dependent on another's judgment of your accomplishments. May you always feel loved.

— Sandra Sturtz

What you truly want out of life
*   cannot be found in the world,*
because what you truly desire,
what you truly long for,
can only be found within yourself.
It does not exist and cannot be found
*   outside of you.*
You must search within your heart,
and not take for granted what
*   your heart offers,*
for it is the only true messenger
*   that you have.*
The heart is the only road paved to
*   fulfillment, happiness, and love.*
For those things that we hold in the
palms of our hands are only as large
*   as that which we can grasp,*
but that which we hold in our hearts
*   is ever increasing,*
*   ever expanding,*
*   forever developing.*
It is as large as the world itself.
That which we hold in our hearts
*   is love . . .*
the only means of life.

— Eugene T. Hewitt, Jr.

*H*old on.

When the day isn't going
  the way that it should;
when there are too many
  clouds in your sky;
when the path you walk along
  takes a turn for the worse . . .

        hold on.

When something you're working on
  doesn't work out;
when it seems there are
  less smiles than frowns;
and just when things seem like
  they're about to fall apart . . .

        hold on.

It's okay to get discouraged,
but don't ever give up.
The sun is always up there
. . . somewhere . . . shining in the sky.

Reach out and do your best
to chase the clouds away.
And remember that every tomorrow
is a whole new opportunity
to begin anew in the light
of a brand-new day.

Just hold on . . . and good things
will surely come your way.

— Collin McCarty

Today Is a New Day

Your tomorrows are as bright
as you want to make them.
There is no reason to carry the darkness
of the past with you into today.
Today is a wonderful new experience,
full of every possibility to make
your life exactly what you want it to be.
Today is the beginning of new happiness,
new directions, and new relationships.
Today is the day to remind yourself
that you possess the power
and the strength you need
to bring contentment, love, and joy
into your life.
Today is the day to be understanding
of yourself,
and to give yourself the love
and patience that you need.
Today is the day
to move forward
towards your bright tomorrow.

— Donna Levine

Make Each and Every Moment of Your Life a Moment to Remember

Be a person who likes virtually everything about life — who is comfortable doing just about anything, and who wastes no time complaining or wishing that things were otherwise • Be enthusiastic about life, and want all you can get out of it • Refuse to worry, and keep yourself free from the anxiety that accompanies worry • Live now, rather than in the past or the future • Seek out experiences that are new and unfamiliar to you • Be strikingly independent • Treasure your own freedom from expectations, and want those you love to be independent, to make their own choices, and to live their lives for themselves • Know how to laugh, and how to create laughter • Accept yourself without complaint • Appreciate the natural world • Enjoy being outdoors in nature and tripping around all that is unspoiled and original • Have insight into the behavior of others, and into yourself, too • *Never feel threatened* • *Engage in work that will make other people's lives more pleasant or tolerable* • *Treat your body well* • *Be honest* • *Have little concern with order, organization, or systems in your life* • *Be creative* • *Love life and all the activities in it* • *Be aggressively curious* • *Search for more to learn each and every present moment of your life* • *Do not be afraid to fail; in fact, welcome it!* • *Do not equate being successful in any enterprise with being successful as a human being* • *Accept others as they are, and work at changing events that you dislike* • *View all people as human, and place no one above yourself in importance* • *Don't chase after happiness; live and happiness is your payoff.*

— Dr. Wayne W. Dyer

*D*on't put off living until tomorrow.
Don't be afraid to dream some time away.
Don't look too far ahead,
   don't look back with regret;
      just look with hope
         to the horizon of today.

Don't be afraid to reach for your goal,
   no matter how distant it might seem.
And don't be surprised if you succeed.

The truly special people in this world,
      the ones who reach their dreams,
   are the ones who do the things
         they really want to do.

Don't be one of the many . . .
   be one of the few.

                    — Collin McCarty

Be someone who knows what you want in life . . .

*N*ot one of us can live merely by knowledge —
you have need to think.
What thoughts are there that you have need of?
You need to think about the true way
of being a human being,
not merely to be someone who has knowledge
or is clever in what he does;
but to be somebody
who knows what he wants to do.
Be one who knows that for life
you require the truth,
that to live you need goodness,
to live you need gratitude;
that within life there is a spiritual life
and that we are but poor if we go into life
without a realization of that spiritual life.

— Albert Schweitzer

Journey towards your dreams

"*B*e what you are,
and become
what you are capable
of becoming."

— *Robert Louis Stevenson*

*E*ach and every one of us
 has the ability to reach out,
   to grow, to change for the better,
   to set our goals and to begin
    traveling in the direction
            of our dreams.

If there is any secret at all
to being happier in life,
it is this:
   to realize what a marvelous
     person you are to begin with;
   to treat that person
     with love and care; and
   to understand that
     if you truly desire for your dreams
     to take you places you've never
     been . . . all you have to do is
      believe in yourself
            . . . and begin.

— Collin McCarty

Take the Time to Do the Things
That Will Bring You Joy

Your life can be happier
if you wake up each morning and give thanks
for having another day to reach
    towards your dreams.
If you share some kind words with your
family and friends,
and listen to what they say to you.
If you spend a moment while you're working
to forgive yourself for any mistakes you
    may have made,
and to forgive those who may have hurt you.
If you keep your thoughts on the things
    you value in life,
and don't worry about what is not important.

If you try to accomplish something
  you've never done before,
because you'll be challenging yourself to grow,
as well as making your life more interesting.
If you do something to make someone happy,
for that person's joy will make you happy.
If you are as true to yourself as you can be,
for your honesty will bring you peace of mind.
If, when you lay your head down to
  sleep at night,
you give thanks once more for the opportunities
you had during the day to achieve and to love.
You can be a happier you
if you take the time to do the things
that will bring you joy.

— *Donna Levine*

*Many people
go from one thing
to another
searching for happiness
but with each new venture
they find themselves
more confused
and less happy
until they discover
that what they are
searching for
is inside themselves
and what will make them happy
is sharing their real selves
with the one they love*

— Susan Polis Schutz

Let Go of the Past

*Let go . . .
of guilt; it's okay to make
the same mistakes again.
Let go . . .
of obsessions; they seldom
turn out the way you planned.
Let go . . .
of hate; it's a waste of love.
Let go . . .
of blaming others; you are
responsible for your own destiny.
Let go . . .
of fantasies; so reality can
come true.
Let go . . .
of self-pity; someone else
may need you.
Let go . . .
of wanting; cherish what you have.
Let go . . .
of fear; it's a waste of faith.
Let go . . .
of despair; change comes from
acceptance and forgiveness.
Let go . . .
of the past; the future is
here — right now.*

— Kathleen O'Brien

Starting today . . .
you can make your life
what you want it to be

Life begins today
and looks forward to tomorrow —
growing, renewing,
beginning again.

It is not what you did
or what you are,
but rather what you will become,
that matters.
For yesterday is gone,
today is here,
and tomorrow will come.

Always look ahead,
leave your pain behind you.
You are the designer
of your own destiny.
You alone can right your own wrongs.
You alone can make peace within yourself.

— Martina Wray Cook

Celebrate Life

*There is a wonderful life waiting to be lived.
Celebrate it today; life is too short to
put off living until tomorrow.*

*Live it fully. Love its changes and choices.
Let it surprise you. Let it show you new ways
of doing old things. Let it help you explore
and discover. Let it introduce you to people
you have never known; to dreams you have never
dreamed; to seeds you have never sown.*

*Let life take away some of your worries and
caress your woes. Let it help you wonder
and laugh and love. Let it show you how to
rise with the sun and aim for the stars.
Let it reveal how to reach out and become
all that you are.*

Let life challenge and encourage you. Let it stimulate and arouse you. Let it embrace and enfold you. Let it show you the majesty of a simple, peaceful morning. Let it show you the miracle of your complexity. Let it help you find your belief and discover your god. Let it amaze you with its possibilities.

Let life help you realize that
it is what you make it, and
that it can be everything
you want it to be.

Have a wonderful day . . .
today and every day.

— Collin McCarty

My Creed

To learn how to live for today.
To understand that I should accept the
things beyond my control, and not take
everything so seriously.
To hold on to courage and hope, and not let
doubt discourage me from doing anything
I aspire to do.
To remember that the world needs the
sunshine of as many smiles as it can get —
and to do my part.
To build bridges instead of walls.
To see the best in others; to acknowledge
their inner beauty with my outer appreciation.
To remember that without friends and loved
ones, my world would be nothing; to be
thankful that with them, it is everything.
To realize that there is an entire lifetime
ahead of me, but precious little time
to be wasted.
To work for my goals, and know that they
can be achieved; and to reach for dreams
with ability, determination and belief.
And finally to know, in the end, that
life will be good to me . . .
if I can do my best
to be good to life.

— Laine Parsons

You Can Succeed

If you go through life
searching for a goal
And you keep searching
until it is found
If you open all the doors
leading to success
And you find happiness
behind each one
If you can raise a smile
to everyone you see
And you hold no grudge
towards anyone at all
If you live each day
to its utmost
And you see things as they are
instead of as they are not
Then you have found
life's truest meaning
And where others have failed
you will succeed.

— Marycarol B. Soistman

If you know
who you are and
what you want and
why you want it
and if you have
confidence in yourself and
a strong will to obtain your desires and
a very positive attitude
you can make
your life
yours
if you ask

— *Susan Polis Schutz*

New Beginnings

*There are times
when we just cannot cope
with what is happening
in our lives.*

*We lose our confidence
easily,
we feel bewildered,
and carry with us a feeling
of disappointment.*

*When we feel like this,
when we are feeling
distressed within ourselves,
we have to learn new ways
for coping with our lives . . .
we have to search
for new beginnings.*

We have to learn
new ways to help us
find peace and contentment
once again;
new ways to help us
make a richer life
for ourselves.

We will never know
just what we can do —
how we can change our lives —
unless we try.

We will never know
until we ask God
to help us search
for a richer life.

And to help us
to start again,
as we make our lives,
if only for a while,
a journey of new beginnings.

— Pauline Smith

You Can Soar Higher than You've Ever Dreamed

Set yourself free from anything that might hinder you in becoming the person you want to be. Free yourself from the uncertainties about your abilities or the worth of your dreams, from the fears that you may not be able to achieve them or that they won't be what you wanted.

Set yourself free from the past. The good things from yesterday are still yours in memory; the things you want to forget you will, for tomorrow is only a sunrise away. Free yourself from regret or guilt, and promise to live this day as fully as you can.

Set yourself free from the expectations of others, and never feel guilty or embarrassed if you do not live up to their standards. You are most important to yourself; live by what you feel is best and right for you. Others will come to respect your integrity and honesty.

Set yourself free to simply be yourself, and you will soar higher than you've ever dreamed.

— Edmund O'Neill

Be the Person You Were Meant to Be

You can be
all of the things you dream of being,
if you're willing to work at them
and if you'll believe in yourself more.
You have a special understanding of people —
why they do the things they do;
why they hurt; why they hurt others.
Learn from the mistakes of others —
accept them; forgive them.
Don't use the roles others have had
in your life as excuses for your mistakes.
Take control, and live your own life.
Continue the journey you've begun:
the journey inside yourself.
It is the most difficult journey you'll ever make,
but the most rewarding.
Take strength from those you love,
and let those who love you help.
Open up your heart; put aside your image,
   and find your real self.
Keep your pride, but don't live for it.
Believe in your own goodness,
   and then do good things.
You are capable of them.

Work at being the you that you want to be.
Sacrifice desires of the moment
*   for long-term goals.*
The sacrifices will be for your benefit;
you will be proud of yourself.
As you approach life, be thankful
for all the good things that you have.
Be thankful for all the potential
*   that you're blessed with.*
Believe in that potential — and use it.
You are a wonderful person; do wonderful things.
True happiness must come from within you.
You will find it
*   by letting your conscience guide you —*
listen to it; follow it.
It is the key to your happiness.
Don't strive to impress others,
but strive to impress yourself.
Be the person you were meant to be.
Everything else will follow;
your dreams will come true.

— Karen Stevens

A Creed for Today and Every Day

Think of the future as a wonderful
*   door opening into a promising new land.*
Learn from the past;
*   but do not let it determine your future.*
Forget about any past mistakes.
Be glad that you are living in a world
*   that is so full of opportunity.*
Be optimistic.
Appreciate the fact that you have God-given
*   talents and abilities that are uniquely yours,*
*   and don't be afraid to use them.*
Be the best you can be.
Seek the advice and help of others,
*   but always remember that*
*   yours is the final word.*
Make your own decisions,
*   explore your own self,*
*   find your own dreams.*
Be persistent;
*   try not to get discouraged when things don't*
*   go your way.*
Do all that you can to make this world
*   a better place to live.*
Be aware that life isn't always easy,
*   but that given time and hard work,*
*   it can be everything you want it to be.*
Most of all, be happy!
The future awaits you,
*   and it's a wonderful time to be alive.*

— Anna Marie Edwards

If ever things begin to look
    a little cloudy . . .
they'll get better soon.
Just remember that it's true:
    it takes rain to make rainbows,
    lemons to make lemonade,
    and sometimes it takes difficulties
    to make us stronger and better people.

The sun will shine again soon . . . you'll see.

— Collin McCarty

ACKNOWLEDGMENTS

We gratefully acknowledge the permission granted by the following authors and authors' representatives to reprint poems and excerpts from their publications.

Marycarol B. Soistman for "You Can Succeed," by Marycarol B. Soistman. Copyright © Marycarol B. Soistman, 1987. All rights reserved. Reprinted by permission.

Karen Stevens for "Be the Person You Were Meant to Be," by Karen Stevens. Copyright © Karen Stevens, 1987. All rights reserved. Reprinted by permission.

Pauline Smith for "New Beginnings," by Pauline Smith. Copyright © Pauline Smith, 1987. All rights reserved. Reprinted by permission.

Kathleen O'Brien for "Let Go of the Past," by Kathleen O'Brien. Copyright © Kathleen O'Brien, 1983. All rights reserved. Reprinted by permission.

Martina Wray Cook for "Starting today . . . ," by Martina Wray Cook. Copyright © Martina Wray Cook, 1987. All rights reserved. Reprinted by permission.

Donna Levine for "Life is our teacher," "You Can Be Whatever You Want to Be," "Today is a New Day," and "Take the Time to Do the Things That Will Bring You Joy," by Donna Levine. Copyright © Donna Levine, 1987. All rights reserved. Reprinted by permission.

Eugene T. Hewitt, Jr. for "What you truly want out of life," by Eugene T. Hewitt, Jr. Copyright © Eugene T. Hewitt, Jr., 1987. All rights reserved. Reprinted by permission.

Albert Schweitzer Foundation, Inc. for "Be someone who knows what you want in life . . . ," by Albert Schweitzer. Copyright © Albert Schweitzer Foundation, Inc., 1987, Glastonbury, CT 06033. All rights reserved. Reprinted by permission.

Dr. Wayne W. Dyer for "Make Each and Every Moment of Your Life a Moment to Remember," by Dr. Wayne W. Dyer from the book, Your Erroneous Zones. Copyright © Wayne W. Dyer, 1976. All rights reserved. Reprinted by permission.

A careful effort has been made to trace the ownership of poems used in this anthology in order to obtain permission to reprint copyrighted materials and to give proper credit to the copyright owners.

If any error or omission has occurred, it is completely inadvertent, and we would like to make corrections in future editions provided that written notification is made to the publisher: BLUE MOUNTAIN PRESS, INC., P.O. Box 4549, Boulder, Colorado 80306.